# Traffic, With Ghosts

**THE HOUGHTON MIFFLIN
NEW POETRY SERIES**

Judith Leet, *Pleasure Seeker's Guide*

David St. John, *Hush*

Heather McHugh, *Dangers*

Gerald Stern, *Lucky Life*

Judith Wright, *The Double Tree:
    Selected Poems 1942–1976*

Christopher Bursk, *Standing Watch*

Thomas Lux, *Sunday*

James McMichael, *Four Good Things*

Reginald Gibbons, *The Ruined Motel*

Maria Flook, *Reckless Wedding*

Tom Sleigh, *After One*

Rosanne Coggeshall, *Traffic, With Ghosts*

# Traffic,
# With Ghosts

Rosanne Coggeshall

WITH AN INTRODUCTION BY
WILLIAM STAFFORD

HOUGHTON MIFFLIN COMPANY BOSTON
1984

2/1985
gen'l

**Library of Congress Cataloging in Publication Data**

Coggeshall, Rosanne, date
  Traffic, with ghosts.

  (The Houghton Mifflin new poetry series)
  I. Title.  II. Series.
PS3553.O4155T7  1984    811'.54    84-10910
ISBN 0-395-36508-2
ISBN 0-395-36509-0 (pbk.)

Printed in the United States of America

Q 10 9 8 7 6 5 4 3 2 1

# Acknowledgments

Certain poems in this collection first appeared in the following publications: *Artemis* — "Reunion" and "Sentenced"; *Caim* — "For John Berryman"; *Carolina Quarterly* — "A Day at the Beach," "Berryman," and "Disbelief"; *Epoch* — "For Annie Dillard"; *Hampden Sydney Review* — "The Prisoner"; *The Hollins Critic* — "The Dead Child"; *Intro I, Intro II* — "The Girl Who Shot the Nuns" and "Emmitt George Is Dead"; *The South Carolina Review* — "Berryman II," "Swim," "For Ross," and "After Reading *Blood, Hook, and Eye*"; *The Southern Poetry Review* — "Janis Joplin"; and *The Southern Review* — "Chain," "Shifts: In Time," "Notice," "News," "An Inland Voice," "Dead Quail," and "Rilke."

"For John Berryman" appeared, in somewhat different form, in *Hymn for Drum* (Louisiana State University Press, 1978).

The lines from "The Fourth Elegy" from *Duino Elegies* by Rainer Maria Rilke, translated by J. B. Leishman, are reprinted by permission of W. W. Norton & Co., Inc., copyright © 1939 by W. W. Norton & Co., Inc., copyright © renewed 1967 by Stephen Spender and J. B. Leishman.

*For my mother and father*
*in memory of my grandmothers*

# Contents

Introduction: Slanging the Language,
*by William Stafford*  xv

## I CHAIN
Chain  3
A Day at the Beach  5
Ditches  7
For John Berryman  9
Berryman  12
Berryman II  13
Hitchhiker  14
Shifts: In Time  16
The Prisoner  18
Notice  19
Janis Joplin  21
The Girl Who Shot the Nuns  23
The Dead Child  24
Emmitt George Is Dead  25
News  26
An Inland Voice  27
Dead Quail  29

## II TENDING THE SUNDAY FIRE
Tending the Sunday Fire  33
Another Sunday Fire  40

## III SENTENCES

Brother Lucas   45
GMH   47
For Now   48
Sentenced   49
The Heart of the Matter   50
Holy Week: 1980   51
Maundy Thursday, 1978   52
A Clear Passage, Struck by Latin   53
Maundy Thursday, 1982   54
Two Pieces   55
Waking   56
Lent, 1982   57
Air That Holds   58

## IV SIMPLIFICATIONS

All Saints' Church, Pawleys Island   63
James Wright (1927–1980)   64
Elegy: Andrew   65
Andrew, Dead   66
For Marlene   67
Swim   68
For a Nephew   69
For Ross   70
The Graduate Student Leaves Home   72
For Ray   73
Mother and Son   74
Mother   75
Reunion   76
After Reading *Blood, Hook, and Eye*   77
Setter   78
For Annie Dillard   79
The Poem   81
Rilke   83
For George Archibald   84
Air   86

**V CLIMBING DEAD MAN:
FOUR VERSIONS AND
A SOLITARY CLIMB**
Climbing Dead Man with Towles   89
Dead Man Alone   93

xiii

# Slanging the Language

## BY WILLIAM STAFFORD

Hopkins and Berryman, and users of slang, have realized that if
you break the language it will often have sharp edges. Rosanne
Coggeshall says, "We got no shoes, but songs are in our fists"; and
"No way is silence / too unsaid to punctuate far praise."

Spring wording and the many hints of drastic presences that
mark the style of this book tease the reader forward, always al-
most *there* with the writer, but always moved off balance again.
And there are other complications.

A Rosanne Coggeshall poem hardly ever seems like a solo. The
declared self is present, but also an unspoken self, nudging the
grammar toward something else, some resonance in the surround-
ings. In these poems a wilderness is waiting outside our houses:
Some things it is better not to mention directly, but not to men-
tion them is to stir them by avoidance. "It's better not to write
like this," one passage says (in "For Annie Dillard"), but the
hovering questions — such as *What? Why?* — are not answered.
The passage goes on:

> But you pass the handle and I grasp it.
> Is there a choice?
> Whose race is it
> and why do we run?

And these questions are followed by simple observations that
begin to be loaded with possible — but never identified —
implications:

> It is Friday.
> It is October.
> It is raining

and I work beside a fire
in a yellow legal pad
without a back, your book
beside last Tuesday's wine.

Passages like this, the parts not enigmatic but the purport
enigmatic, haunt the book. Sometimes the note of strangeness
comes from inserted lines deliberately set off and left to reverber-
ate, as in the two italicized lines in "Sentenced":

*I wait only and ever*
*for the one door's dissolution.*

Another world waits behind the poems, a world not quite men-
tioned but all too real.

Amid the steady reassurances of life — and some of these poems
have that air of reassurance ("Air That Holds," "All Saints'
Church, Pawleys Island") — we are made to realize that security
exists only so long as the senses are tuned for that condition: If
our senses were tuned higher, our surroundings would always be
full of surprises. And sometimes that additional environment
shudders forward, as in the ending of "For John Berryman":

Words are wells in which we drink or swim.
Their mirror skins hold rings for saving.
Ice does figure in.
Henry, I would rather say,
go cross the bridge.
The fatherest far is not too edge.

Some of the acrobatics in a passage like that will serve to warn
that those fit for scrambling in language, and those with a back-
ground of information, will receive much more from this book
than will those who read by knowing dictionary definitions only.
Some of the strides in these poems are long strides.

But going through the poems will teach the way to go; separate
pages are parts of a bigger story, or are like glints on a shield
partly obscured. Though the onwardness of the telling in each
poem prevents any stopping to explain, the reader leans forward,
because the elucidations light up from the individual brilliance
of the episodes.

How does the language take on its glitter? One way is by jumbling together separate developments at a pace faster than the usual transitions would lead us to expect. A verse paragraph from "For John Berryman" has this kind of pace:

> I never had a daughter   no.
> But I drank laughter with my dog
> until she left, beautiful woman
> is her name, she's gone.
> Rope hangs heavy in the hand
> that hooped the rain.

These revved-up transitions animate a passage that enlivens with hints of formal poetry, as sounds jostle each other, but not in their usual places in stanzas — daughter-laughter, woman-name, and gone-hangs-hand-rain.

Many ghosts inhabit these pages, but there is other traffic as well. Out of this various traffic Rosanne Coggeshall steers us to such balance as we human beings can attain. Refusing easy claims, she says, in "Dead Man Alone,"

> Yet even in denial
> heart and blood respond.
> Levels in me
> rarely warmed by weather's light
> shift, rescind
>
> as the small oak
> in William's meadow
> takes its branches up
> and weaves the wind.

# I Chain

# Chain

For EHC (1907–1973)

Today I wore your willed gold chain
to court. Tried again and guilty once again
I paid the sixteen dollars asked
for accidentally saving lives.
*Yours I lost too suddenly:*
*every summer feature gone.*

Stuck words stick still.
But now you will me
into making up another chain,
a chain of linking letters
that invoke the kinning blood,
the blood that made me
your last sister's child;
and while, willed, words refuse,
or, worse, abuse themselves
and others by the silences
they recognize as more,
I tear up letters, birthday cards,
boxes bearing your return address,
because of what I cannot say.

Today the chain that you once wore
encircled my mute throat.
It held me through the lists
of strangers who had stronger reasons
to be anywhere but there,

where I,
who cannot die,
sat wordlessly
and shook,

not looking at the faces
of the auntless
and the bold.

## A Day at the Beach

The Jewish rye is gone.
We drive the twenty minutes
to the store
and do not speak
the single word
the dear know
saves the day.

Market made of people
*and the lamppost leans*
*again the victim*

I think
my head
is shrinking
to
a tulip bulb

*Light changes*

I have charged
the sauerkraut        the beer
the Jewish rye        and more.
Behind your breath
you swear
because your mother
gave you ample warning
in the womb:
*Beware*
*beware*
*the girl with glass for anger*
*a cistern for a heart*

5

Together in the yellow car
we watch the white lines stretch
to keep us straight.

*Mouth moving under will*
I tell you that the silver vine
has strangled your last risk
of flowers.

Later, in the middle room,
beneath salt sheets
I hear the gulls
go down:
silence shifts
between the waves

and the lives
of shells
we never looked for
still go on.

## Ditches

I sit beside the ditch
while cars go by.
Released seven hours, maybe more,
wearing shoes that never fit, I sit,
curved and folded, like the Indian
lost tribe brothers ride the range to kill.

I draw a gun on my left hand
with a broken bottle neck, after careful aim;
it is the same: the fire, the small-cased letter
brought by the nurse in yellowed shoes,
the one the trees have all betrayed.
"oh," I read again, "i would have stayed
had autumn been less clear,
the leaves less cold and sharply drawn.
i would have gone to any depth
to surface in your glass,
that simple glass you carry
in your arm's lost crook,
the place you look for
when you find you're lost."

I discover on my wrist small half-moon scars.
Symmetrical, they form a larger half-moon scar,
and I, myself, first arm, then body, bend
into a moon's wrong half,
the insufficient part of lesser light,
the insufficient start of whole.

Spooling by the cars have no effect.
I have walked — or I will walk —
down to the harbor
where smoke-thick factories horizon
every look to sea;
where we, explosives trapped
in unconsidered spring, would wander,
bringing on our backs dead gulls
and skulls of reptiles you had killed
the desert year you lost your son.

The ditch my face is bottomless and calm.
I wander, I am still, I wake again to kill
the harmless bird, the gull the sea refused.
And no, abused I've never been:
the window that you built
has never held real glass.
Empty now, as then, it shows me
how the world looks back
unsought, unrecognized, and rare.
The earth wears trees and ditches like old scars.

My hands the stars refuse the threshold of a word.
In case you never heard I will not speak,
and you may take or leave the silence,
for all or nothing, as you please.

# For John Berryman

### I

Two nights the dog has roomed in rain,
beautiful and red. Simple grow
the sleeves of this old shirt.
Dust forms windows in the floor.
Henry's book hurt, helped, it's more.
Somewhere she is curling into sleep.
Not too rainy, Henry, not too deep.

I never had a daughter    no.
But I drank laughter with my dog
until she left, beautiful woman
is her name, she's gone.
Rope hangs heavy in the hand
that hooped the rain.

### II

Henry, I have finished your sad songs
and they are    mostly    sad
and songs to    here    around the wrinkle
of a chord that grows a muscle
and is strong: chords of wrists reck
blood and buckle into breath
that feathers flutes.
Show me someone sings
I show you bones that float.

But your bones bit ice.
I wonder which broke first.
The sick grow lame in aim, I think;
sick. But only silver hacksaws tell.
I wall easily. Glass grows emptily
in twos   in threes. But   Henry
there are trees in the window,
there are trees.

## III

Afterwards we all run out and cheer.
We take chalk and draw a polar bear
on that steep night. They tell us:
leave Henry Pussycat alone: he dead:
he deeper than the stone's lost blood.

We got no shoes, but songs are in our fists.
We all wear sweat like bandages and fly,
oh Henry we do fly with wings
and hold the hemisphere in spoons,
in saucers, cups. No way is silence
too unsaid to punctuate far praise.

## IV

Henry, now is like a gas gauge empty gone,
lets us fill with slippery sleep,
does not come when called, but, hid from,
pounces, ravishes. *Dream again*
*of the lost Maud suppling into fields.*
*Cellos play. Somebody reads.*
You are deader than the door my dog controlled.
I have welded all your verbs into a wheel
that wasn't closed and won't,
just rolls and rattles,
but it rattles sweet.

I can't let the letter die like this:
so unspoked, unholy. Henry,
we are fully now a piece.
When I wear the shirt it has two holes.
Words are wells in which we drink or swim.
Their mirror skins hold rings for saving.
Ice does figure in.
Henry, I would rather say,
go cross the bridge.
The fatherest far is not too edge.

## Berryman

It is not so long now Henry
since the dive was won
and you or I released the small beast
from the paper box and turned
so's not to watch him as he fled.
They said you died, but I found

a nearer tree and my old brown dog Ham
and whittled with him through two nights
until an unlit star struck near us
in the ground. Descending I could find
a nickel pot and that torn gray scarf
one of us would wear when waking

in a far walk after dream before the dawn
slipped in. When Ham ran with me much ahead,
they said in papers you were not.
I found steps more difficult,
working incomprehensible.
In this tree I wander     limb
to limb.

I don't go down.
Instead I free
each furred or feathered clump
I happen on. If I forget now ever
that you're not     I may climb down
but not now, Henry,
not in this spliced dawn.

## Berryman II

By Bunsen burner he wracked word on word
until the *Songs* stretched longer than a year
with thrice as many midnights    hardly any noons.

Croon he could to his heavy daughter;
her heft lifted him.
But trafficked too plentifully with ghosts:
*witchman*
*switchman*
*sluggerman*
*poor:*

poorer maybe than we know
with his shook soul    his missioned heart.

Called *curtain* at last
assuming inheritance
his latest prance:

grieved himself into deep grave
to save the hacked-up face
from more regular ruin.

# Hitchhiker

Because you kept your crucifix concealed
and never spoke of absolution, I rode
your silence hours on end,
each hour a boxcar, the same
but oddly shaped, packed
secretly with stolen good.

I said my name. You sat still.
I told you I had killed my mother
and her nurse. You never flinched.
I told how illness crept into her palms
and turned them black, how she could
only muffle prayers and hold the tears:
*like cellophane her eyes.*
I said the ways we bind ourselves
to houses is remote; to meet
your mother in a darkened room,
to bear her ghost,
is wild enchanting incest.
You driving on said nothing.

If I had known the highway well
I would have fallen from the truck
and waked myself to run.
By then the sun had disappeared,
the stars, cold weapons, threatened
to unite and press into me
till I shrieked, confessed, revoked.
Spoken, your words, *torn cloth,*
said evenly that death too had a middle name
that sounded in the dusk like water falling
in a well: the sound of nothing

14

falling into nothing, a rigid lift
of laughter at the edge.

I got out at the bridge.
Between us glass and metal,
narrow sentences, and quiet.
Like a rock I hulked
inside the bridge's clay.
I tried to breathe the water rhythm
as it lasted black away.

## Shifts: In Time

For AF and PS


He said the slugger said:
"I ain't got much time.
I ain't got time for bases
so I gots to hit this ball
as far as Kansas, far
as Sally's house in South Carolina
where the moss drops down."

        *much time:*
        *is:*
        *nothing*
*much*

   My sisters never fought
   and when the lady died next door
   we all wore nylon socks and shoes
   and took fresh flowers for her porch.
   I put my jonquil on the joggling board
   and looked between the window lace
   to see if Milk the puppy still was
   eating rhododendrons in the hall.
   He wasn't there. From where I stood
   I only saw the mirror and the stairs
   that curved until they disappeared.

   One Easter morning when my brother's cow
   got lost, we walked the pasture
   until noon, missing all of church.
   At dinner when my father said the prayer
   I wore my napkin on my head and no one said
   a word.

16

I caught a bird one Saturday that June
with buckshot in its wing. I kept it
in a Mason jar until the glass turned black.

A boat I saw in Maryland
the August I was five
had seven sails and silver circles
in its side; the water hid
the bottom,
but I could tell
it too
curved down
to
disappear.

Today I can't remember if the dogs are fed
or if the bed's been made this month.
*Time works wonders,* so the bottle says.

*Nights and days the slugger slugs*
*and misses every pitch.*
*His days are numbered.*
*Which is which*
*he doesn't know*
*to know.*

## The Prisoner

My ghost passes out without a nod.
Where I'm hidden
all light is made of ash
and sifts apart
when the wind shifts.

If anybody dares
to lift this lid
I'm cold afraid
my bones will drift up
silver,
single,
ready to catch fire.

# Notice

Often
that October,
when light spun
shadows through
the sycamores
beside the kitchen door,
we built an early fire,
and pulled the rockers
to the hearth,
warm drinks in hand.

Brazilli, bless her teeth,
had left us then,
and every day the stack
of dishes grew until
I feared they'd topple
with the closing of a door.

Still,
afternoons,
those late ones
by the fire,
we'd take the album
from the shelf
and look again
at what had come to what.

The day the notice came
the barn door had been unhinged
a week; those cows were everywhere.
Instead of looking out
or looking down again

19

to read the crystal words
that marked directions
that our palms would have to take,
I called the puppy and the goat
and walked a long time out beyond
the pond to the place
the trees took over
and let go.

# Janis Joplin

## I

If, at a well, she had come
to Jesus, standing, thristy,
it would not have been a question
then of speech; she would have reached,
dropped bucket, dipped for him
the silent, undemanded answer.
And he, then, drinking, silent,
would have locked the recognition in.

Then later, never understanding,
bending under beaten branches, beaten leaves,
she would have raised the slim forked wrists,
lifted severed voice, longing simply
to the moon.

## II

Something walked her inner arm,
stalking blue lines,
tracking to the heart its prey,
the subtle beat that beat unstudied,
regular and ruined;
high-pitched, high-tuned
to smash the glass,
to tear the dog's ear, mouth to teeth,
grounding breath to hunt.

## III

Somewhere beneath a rhythmed fist
it moves to that: the simple need
for ear to fast, to hunger, fastened
to the leaning moon: Actaeon wounded,
wound in woman's flesh; and yet not flesh
nor woman hunted, but the memory of song,
the long, raw cry that rises
wordlessly to mark discovery, the kill.

# The Girl Who Shot the Nuns

From her third-story window
they looked like penguins, cold and comic,
shuffling through the snow.
She didn't know their names, their come or go,
or what black ghost had tricked them
of their hair and the share
of a warm-sheeted bed. But still,
she wished them dead.

She raised her long-nosed gun,
aimed at the broadest one
whose motherlap slid smoothly in the wind.
The fat bird jerked
and fell face flat against the snow.
The slower sister turned to scream
when gleaming barrel
blew her breast to blood.

Above, the sniper stood,
nose against the screen,
and watched black shadows
stain the clean white snow.
She didn't know if they were dead,
and later said that she supposed them
coming up from prayer,
or going there.

# The Dead Child

*Who'll show a child just as it is . . .*
*who'll make its death from gray bread,*
*that grows hard, or leave it there,*
*within the round mouth, like the choking core*
*of a sweet apple . . . death, the whole of death,*
*— even before life's begun, to hold it all so gently,*
*and be good: this is beyond description.*

— Rainer Maria Rilke, *The Fourth Elegy*


He is blue now.
From gray, mold took him
hardening the arms, the spindle legs,
changing him
to blue.

He stood, bare-faced and open,
stood and held it all in seed-small teeth,
held until he became both tooth and seed,
unnatural and soft beneath the molding hand,
clay replaced by living bread,
made and molded, gray to distant blue.

And you, apart, back on your heels,
accuse the air made broad with grief.
Startled into finding in a leaf
something other, more than green,
you turn from what you've seen
with open shudders, wondering at wind.

And he, the small, the smallest friend
of many-fingered death, holds still,
grips the living apple
in the small blue teeth.

24

# Emmitt George Is Dead

For Arie

In the belly of a bomber
fire digested him, dissolved the marrow
of his bones to dust
and spat him,
ashes to the wind.

My friend, his mother, sweeps the kitchen floor,
bakes corn bread, irons my father's shirts.
Death hurts her still,
and her yellowed eye

rounds and brims when a jet breaks by.
But Jesus hems her hollows
when she rips the hymns
from yellow keys her Emmitt cracked.

Grief-stiffened faith is stacked
in pillars in this room
where her broom sniffs
quietly, pushing dust around.

# News

The family sat, ate porkchops,
crackling bread, drank milk
instead of tea or wine:
they dinnered quietly.
Once or twice the youngest fell
to the floor, fit-tied to laughter.
The farmer's daughter washed the dishes
afterwards, swept the kitchen floor.
She wore her shadow down,
she covered up her shadow
with her shadowed self, fell,
struck blind, mindless in a dream
blown out of poison
and the sinking mud of swine.

It's not over.
Covered in the news
are two who still survive.
The mother lives:
beneath her apron moves,
sometimes, a creature
stranger than the shadow of her doubt
that when we play at prayer,
at making good the food we eat,
sometimes there festers in the meat
raw husks of grain
too hidden to be blessed.

## An Inland Voice

I do not know the place.
They say it's small,
mere shoetongue in the sea,
her island off the coast of Georgia.

I am sixty-three, six summers older
than my sister, who keeps geese, I hear,
and sucks her thumb.

Once, years ago, we walked
the dust trail up the meadow
from the chapel where our father preached
and came, not noticing, upon a green snake
stiffly curved into its death.
Around our patent shoes were darker shadows
of two birds who flew in rings
above the straw that, circling,
made our hats.

I don't remember what she said;
simply that I dropped my hymnal,
ran without another glance
at that dark ritual
moving at my feet.

She lives, or so they tell me,
in a cottage in the middle of that island
with just the geese
and photographs I send each May
of Father's garden
in the spring.

The meadow with the path was sold
ten falls ago; the old tin roof
where rain hit, bare music's bones,
is torn back from the barn.
The cows are gone.

I do not live with shadows.
The lamps he left are bright
and, overhead, the chandeliers
are clear of cobwebs; light
spills simply, spans the edges
of each separate room.

# Dead Quail

The sky cracked.
A piece fell. A flapping piece
with feathers and dark blood.
Wind parted when it fell;
grass opened, closed, and from it
rose a silence dark as blood.
I stood behind and watched the wind
move feathers back to life.
A leaf blew up, stuck against the moving blood,
I stood behind and waited for the ghost to give.
I wouldn't leave. It hovered like the bird it was.
Does this mean something, said the wind.
Does this mean nothing, said the grass.

The feathers lived against the losing blood.
The grass stood back, the sounding wind.
Send the ghost away, they said, the quail is dead.
They spoke together. Feather moved in blood
and still I watched, waiting for the ghost.

At last the blood was black and didn't move.
The feathers turned to sticks.
I was left behind
as wind divided for the ghost;
as grass first opened, silent,
and then, silent, closed.

# II Tending the Sunday Fire

# Tending the Sunday Fire

## I

I tend the Sunday fire:
rhymeless care, care woebegone
against warmth's risk and light,
loosely trained, lost syllables,
long languages of smoke.

There is no match in unwilled
structure, sycamore and oak, elm
elbow, fist of spruce; kindling
spent now, blades of flame carve
color from rent air.

I am here again
too long about warmth's invocation.

Criminal cold clamps shadows to the floor.
I've fed the puppies, bolted door and window
against Eucharist of memory,
taut alphabet of loss.

Afternoon up on the ridge
I saw the cove sheer silver —
islands everywhere like straits —

and now to settle, subtle
out a place.
I ply treepieces with my pilgrim crook
and trace ash hieroglyphs
for answer, question, reason
not to rail.

*No light*

but in this heat
a wandering of gold,
sun stored and wooded,
drawn to tides;
sun told.

**II**

Reading of a dead man's lust
I quarter meter, stare to fire
more actual than real. Younger,
I too seared blood in bother
for another scythe, for one more
lesion home. I wore
welts in my wrists, reaching.

Now cohesion's torn
in memory's vise.
Outside chain saws threaten,
trucks downshift.
Something I never left
loses me, here in this strait
where pages blank in wooded light,
and night, more certain now
than quick, clasps over all
its threaded, hemless cowl.

**III**

Hearthed
I am at home
with fire-split wood,
oak-opened rhythm,
sun's color, water's depth.
You are in your castle.

All's well in distance, too.
Mostly now
I celebrate the ghosts:
pasts too syndicated
to refuse.
Your denial
from sound throne
discovers
only
that this hearth
is unfamiliar, finally,
this fire as wanton
as it is ingrown.


## IV

A Jehovah's Witness risks
the holey road to bring
the news of Christmas Two.
I listen as I lean to see
her Rabbit, blue and gold.

Her second coming lends
new roughage for the fire,
new damage to undo in me.
*Over all of this,*
*beyond belief,*
I grieve a loss
less lofty.

Let us meet upon this gently,
I want to say;
let's halve toast, share tea.
But Eucharist between us
would mean no more
than any thing
unravelled as it's done,

practiced only
in the incidence
of absence
too fretted
to absolve.


## V

Hottest now
with gold red bottom
and a lace of blue,
this Sunday fire can figure me.
Windows lost, reflection glass,
I can move
only in expense of air.

Outside ice temples
every lane; ice rain stuns grass,
crystallizes leaves.
Far before me mountains
mist away
through ice in air.

Everywhere I look
things stiffen, shine;
ornamental drapery
in foliage chimes;
I breathe ice air
and chill
inside: resolution;
monarchy; a season
to abide.

Weather through the window,
weather of my heart,
return themselves
each to the other.

In all the stir
another day unhinges, another hour
tolls sere.

## VI

This fire needs no attention —
three birch knots, a cross of oak.
Heat's spool unbinds and I rock back,
thirsty, mostly known.
Patterns in my wrist spell
other countries, targets there and time.
I watch smoke separate;
I rue another rhyme,
see

you on a back street
hometowned, free;
children in your shadow
find your hands.

Who doesn't know
the scrolls we leave
in faces, in each palm,
would wish for distance
less profound;
another separation
not so fraught
with repetition's signature,
the skewed name,
*remorse.*

## VII

There is no Sunday fire.
Morning sprockets night's last leaves,
and dimensionless we enter
another sun's dilemma.

37

Canyons now go floorless:
bottom land means treachery
in treachery.
Trees scar themselves
in winds no one can see
and you with me collect
white stones and wait.

I could never write of this
beside the Sunday fire.

Outside, in fields pressed winter flat,
I light a cigarette, attendant on the dawn.
In violet apprehension
no fire long gone can indicate
air's harsh, air's wildest warmth.

## VIII

Vertical
the horizontal logs,
birch, beech, elm, and oak,
turn fire
between themselves,
divide
up smoke.

I listen to the air transforming,
spent.

In this down-slanted light,
crossed by its own worst loss,
I see no intersection.
This fire intends far more
than woodstruck beings
can say.

Pretend as I might,
I can only claim
singular warmth,
and want, desire
of you
against expense
of night.

# Another Sunday Fire

There are several ways to kindle wood.
I can tell you neither what I know
nor what I think: only that rain
speaks through these trees.
It falls straight, like shot.

Woodsmen make fires easily;
thoughtless in habit, they treat
the time impartially, minutes
in a row.
Mothers, who must split wood
then make from it provision
for the day, look out through windows long with dust;
they strive, too,
imageless,
lost, too, in abdicated space.

In the rain, derelicts court fire:
deprivation begets despair
in the long cough towards sleep.
Drunks heat soup on flames bred up
from newsprint, paper bandages, leaves.
In any moment, one might somersault
outside fire's arc, strangled
by his own unwillingness to dream.

There are other ways;
there are casualties, loss.
It rains now in Cypress Woods
and in the tent beside my self

I see smoke spring off
erratically and hear the fire
I woke to make
go on
despite these absences of rule.

# III    Sentences

## Brother Lucas

Penciling the creeds
on his cell's door,
he envisions Christ
in shawled surplice
just beyond the stair.

Brother Lucas found a star
in his robe pocket
when Father turned his head.
He fixed it to the windowsill,
said nothing to his brothers
down the hall.
He called it Spiritus,
bled himself before it nightly;
paled and weakened to a shade.

Brother Lucas saw his sight
diminish and depart;
he never wept; he prayed
he might see sharper
in the dark.
Certainly his work
grew steadier, brighter
than before.

Upon his door creeds cross
and intertwine.
Somewhere near the line where men
affirm the sacred Ghost
a constellation streams —

fast proof of schemes
more hidden
than the dreams of wild beasts
asleep in tangled straw.

# GMH

Of prayer he understood that only sheer
Risk made nerve new, glinted, sere.
Knees notched, by rock, glass, shale,
Lean face a glossary to grief,
When he hammered heart, he hammered rail
To hinged things: the startled leaf,
The awful whyness of us all.
No matter how he felled he struck the toll
Rebattered under his own trialed chest.
Mountains miled with light, stern splints,
Removed for him in bright erratic slants,
Returned the plain wholed glory Christ
Caught calvaried and steep.
He recognized starred rescue crossed in deep.

47

## For Now

Even you
at your back door
pinning moths to light
know avalanche when you glimpse it,
know tornado, draught.

Space without rim invokes you,
balances unwary —
*tins of needles, Judas wings.*

Nails you know and cleavers,
split penance, vagrant ties.
But when you give the baker your address,
never does it cross your mind
that in the loaf
may be a richness of martins,
a feathering of snow,
two gremlins locked in an embrace.

What you know you know.
Still, when your gaze finds the window,
your screen against ravage,
you see your only shield your face.

# Sentenced

Listen.
All around you
little bones are cracking,
feathered bodies blister into flight;
all around you eggs heal
and lichen, like skin, draws white.

*I wait only and ever*
*for the one door's dissolution.*
Hinges happen anywhere,
but the solid startled plank
stands singular and blank.
Knock, scrape, kick as you do,
entrance is denied.

      Stand as you do
on the seasoned side of breath,
you can only lean eastward into wind
and keep your hemmed heart
arched.

## The Heart of the Matter

Often at your desk
you look over the edge
and there see
narcissus, dogwood, juniper,
and thyme. Now
while sun's down and towns everywhere
brittle out in lassoed light

you must
watch a little
that cabin windowed white,
there across the bean field,
where rose grows high
and wintergreen threads sage,
the torn new moon
at odds
in a tangled sky.

# Holy Week: 1980

Up and down the interstate
bald tires break; feet need washing
in every county soled in dirt.
Great Truths: Holy Week, Good Friday.
The story is the same,
pillages its own while in
the severaled heart
its blood goes stone.

*No thirst so deep could last,*
*no templed eye could fast,*
*fixed so upon outrageous nails,*
*the placid wood.*

If this day is wholly good
no other sunrise can survive
the treachery of prayer,
broad witlessness of vision,
that brutal sphere
pure air.

# Maundy Thursday, 1978
### For VBF


Before the triple stained glass windows
he and he enact
the washing of the feet.

From where I sit
I see only rounded backs,
collars, white rims capping
shouldered dark.

Before me ritual incarnates.
Gesture symbol lesson emblem
sacrament encode:
last supper to be made
here, for those of us
whose hands are clasped,
whose grasps will hold us
so we too can thread
our unwashed ways
up to the front,

hoping to believe
our own massed motions
long enough to later find
the porch with one rimmed light,

the light
we turn out
when the dark
we move through
is our own.

52

## A Clear Passage, Struck by Latin

For Anna


Latin — is it trickery?
To make you
screw your vision
down
to tarnished point,
despair.

We read word, sentence;
nod, know.
Then: Latin.

Antiquity, obliquity:
can mystery stand
so simply hid?
We all watch scandal
now and then
and call it grace.

Once, on an autumn morning,
five rapt mallards
flung a pattern
round a house near Tinker Creek.
Inscrutable, the message;
but the medium was air.

# Maundy Thursday, 1982

For Bishop William deJ. Rutherfoord


In the margin of Paul's book
you've drawn Christ crucified.
Upon the cross,
a figure
scrawled;
a jagged S,
he bleeds.

      As I read
my eyes leap
contexts
language-bound
into
a wilderness so rare
I have to know:

This is death:
death essential, death laid bare;
our Father's farthest son,
the man for whom
all others are undone.

## Two Pieces

**I**

The random air
approves nothing
like this October wedge:
light worked out of leaves,
an intricacy of gilt,

*gold,*

more gold
than an egg's heart
split
and spilled:

let go.

**II**

Morning is like this:

fine edge of light
strains out of dullness,
the quick-shored tremble
of crimson,

the heart
a streak away.

## Waking

After EEC

When night's noose slips
over everything that hinges
riddled air,
apples' sphere
of heaviness hangs on.

Sometimes then
a mockingbird will lose its place
and start a morning piece,
and I alone in my severaled midst
will track a prayer
to a woven breeze.

*Nowhere, not even in memory,*
*have there been such trees.*

# Lent, 1982

For CRB

Across the calendar
I trace days' passage.
Every hour stuns rest.
Abandoned by old sanities,
Old sense, I resurrect
the unkept ghost of morning,
this season without tense.

    You in another room
weave weapons.
I have no name for what I shield.

If Christ cut himself free
to cross out my iniquity,
I must baffle small betrayals
of my soul's worst self.
If prayer were easier,
words in my wake could wick
atonement, indicate a light.

    By the fire your handiwork
reflects a sailor's bond;
careful stitches bind
through ash's fall.
Warmth like dust spins up,
visible.

*I can intend no sanctity,*
*no relinquishment of awe.*

## Air That Holds

Under hood of ash
you pitch about and pray:
every morning, every afternoon.
You're climbing Jacob's ladder
on your knees,
seven days a week.
You think:
*to dance is better—*
*whirl praise, leap gratitude—*
but knees bend, wrists lock.
You can only kneel.

One night you dream of hummingbirds.
They silver at your window,
voices human, hinged.
They speak of Christ
as if he were the crust
that made their blood;
and as they speak they hang
in air
that holds them
where they are.

When you awake
you walk from the house
to the field's edge
where you stand,
waiting,
air against you
like another dream.

No matter how you turn
or where,
*you find an answer,*
*you find an answer*
*there.*

# IV  Simplifications

# All Saints' Church, Pawleys Island

On Waccamaw River All Saints' tries
the ancient woods for rest.
Against those woods the tidal creek
revises currents from the sea;
and sea, beyond, invades the air
and trees themselves thread wind
to streams.

All Saints' windows believe all light.
Salt crystals shine
and sun in whirlwinds
pushes dark around.

## James Wright (1927–1980)

For Tommy Thompson

Tom remembers
a solid, word-wrung man,
dark-suited at a table,
hands out like pale plates,
offering.

*Did he seize time's throat*
*too nearly?*
*Did he loosen rust?*
*Or was it for the water:*
*did there his pity strum too wide?*

Tom knows the music
never heard but read;
from centered silence
he works out the phrase.

*Whatever weathers wield him,*
*there waters' seal*
*turns air.*

# Elegy: Andrew

That night we hunched together on the step,
shared sherry from a flask
(our common plot to outwit fear),
night tore me down.

*Night:* your schismed heart;
the shirt you wore
to screen the scar.

Pulled back by a quirk of air
I'm there again,
beside you with the wine our share
but not our only bond by far.

Brother, death didn't spare you
your complex doom.
A scar like a spur
marked the treasure,
pillaged, spent.

## Andrew, Dead

pronounced trounced
on survival
fought not
for fright of shatter.

Woke laced in sweat
punctually each night
when chimes halved in seacoast chapels
seconding themselves.

Wrenched from air
enough
to cut it out
of his routine.

Remorse ripped up his wake.
Shreds crop up still
in bolted studies
with windows that front
water
or
stunned land.

## For Marlene

You say poems mean
only when they're thrown,
like clay, or formed
of stuff visible,
"real."
You notch fall in light and color
in the world of separation
or of rain,
spun so it's single
like a cover, vertically shook.

Maybe you write down
how open
air can be in autumn
when rain in colors carries down
the dust. Maybe
you say October halves the wind.

Or you might notice apples,
split in sores, or pears
too brown to rot; or sumac
in the arched hall of a wood.
What you see you say,
and saying you can see
how long a sentence is
that opens with an eye.

# Swim

I slit Black Creek
with my own aimed hands
my own primed hull.

It seals itself above me
simply as I pull
into its current
and head across
toward the flat smooth stone
below the bend.

Under its sleek skin
I mend steep absences,
tend creek motion with my own,
until we recognize each other
one more year for good.

My body loosens,
offers its paired pieces
to the stream, exchange
for the carved prize,
the mansioned prize,
the prize for reatonement

with the land's one vein
that held and blooded me,
that charged my newest hinges
with the word:

*wings restore themselves*
*when air returns*
*to flood.*

68

## For a Nephew

For an hour
on the pier
we skip flat stones,
cut water;
bright slashes scatter.
You know where they go.

Not long ago I tilted you
in my arms away from August sun.
Your hands like stars
split random air
and in your hair
I smelled the sea wind rise.

While you grew
hemispheres away
I drew pictures every day
of a small boy
caught in distance
at dance
with the sea.

## For Ross

Ross is afraid of tornadoes.
I am too.
Once, as I was driving to the island,
the radio warned
of tornadoes in the county.
I ditched the car
and ran two miles in rain
to an old house where older people
gave me tea and stale dry biscuits,
never asking why I'd come.

And I didn't tell.
Tornadoes suddenly became
unsprung and easy
in my mind.
I found the couple
knew my father's aunt,
had cousins buried
in my family's ground,
knew everything there is to know
about old pottery
and chess.

Hours later
I walked dark fields
to find my car.
Stars were stuck
In every shadow overhead;
dead 'possums glared
with starry eyes.
I thought of Ross;

I tried to tell him
in my head
that fear
can be displaced.
I traced the old man's face
in my mind's bend

and drove the hundred miles
to Pawleys in clear silence,
looking up at clouds
and little lights
that told of something other,
close,
beyond.

# The Graduate Student Leaves Home

For LDS

Time zones away
you probably shelve books
or watch your husband wind
his watch before he means goodbye.
Boxes around you threaten permanence,
possession you can't will or count
as loss.
Unfamiliar windows place things
where they are and you hear
your own voice
in another house,
making do
with silence.

When you watch, new dust
will pull back, mazed.
New, the walls will meet
in corners where new lights
split space.

Distances try numbers
at the numbers' bones.
When ought's divided
finitude's untitled;
spaciousness can spin the zones.

## For Ray


I drive to Fincastle
with the lights on
though the sun still balances
on Dead Man
like an orange.

Signs warn of bends,
broad curves, quick drops;
houses draw back, turn
small in my wake.

In the end I pull
up behind the ancient church
and go inside to hear
a lady tell me God is good.
Because she tells me,
I wear the hour well,
I find the way back home
against my will,
all signs reversed,
Dead Man's shoulder
like a dark comforter
under petaled sky.

# Mother and Son
### For Cece

Your afternoon kitchen:
sun in glass
and on the floor like paint;
you memorize the hour of him,
there,
sitting on the counter,
reading jars.

Now,
when around him nothing stuns
and he alone is shocking
in the still air,
you lean against severance,
torn land defined.

If
years ago,
your brackets tendered
for release, if
then you'd read
blood's inverse toll,
you might have borne
no sterner version
of your own true startled heart,
but some one other —

not this caution,
this crown of bothered hair,
this bowed attention to these names
of things too certain surely
to be likely known
or rare.

74

# Mother

### For Anna

Her arms from sun took color
that worked light to skin,
and in her hands were hatchets
and a home.

Never was care steeper.
Brute devotion turned scholar
in her heart's hem.

Not till mother-whelming made her
more than she'd feared become;
not till scythes and nails, harpoons and helmets
sickled her
and the moon itself (spurred discus, worried hive)
struck round;
not till then
could she bend through herself in time enough to shadow,
to let shadow
have its second length of love.

## Reunion

They fly in tonight from the south.
They bring with them hidden bones,
blood primed to liven, flesh, hair,
teeth: the works.
The works they bring they are:
pen wielders, word bearers, clock haunters,
glancers, ghosts: mother, father.

I watch the coiled sun center
against the witlessness of sky.
I have wanted to touch there,
that rift in air,
to feel fire that clean,
known distance
in an arc.

They see it too,
are closer.

When they land
deep shadows, interrupted,
will close on plane silver.
Steps down
will seem
steeper,
the ground itself
a fall.

# After Reading "Blood, Hook, and Eye"

For Dara Wier

## I

Sometime other I threw books from trains.
In front of me two women in calico
cut up potatoes, told each other lies.
One said her husband wore a harpoon
through his shoulder like a badge.
I peeled an apple, ate the skin and stem.

This afternoon between walks
I read your sentences in rows.
Inside of me silence grows wider,
with more pockets
for keepsakes, tourniquets;
for tools.

## II

You wrote it differently.
Your soles roughened
over shards I never saw.
Somewhere in your distance
trains passed and people on them
swapped pumpkin seeds, lenses
from microscopes, pencils cut
from beech.

Nowadays I watch out for cars.
In them, something's going on.
I dream up conversations between mothers,
over coffee, in the sun.

77

# Setter

Ginny

As I move, cold separates and closes,
cleaves to my face like stain:
thin bones of ice craze leafcover
and the dog shivers,
her breath a scoop of cloud.

She's made to run
and running she peels free
of ground rigidity,
becomes sole citizen of air,
scion of hurricane,
fur ethereal,
lighter than stripped pine.

Spanning speed and distance
she denies air edges
that hit earth to stick.
Motion quickens deepest blood.
Body looses heft to sheen.

At the hill's cleft
below the bend
I watch her touch
each scaffold
in ice wind.

## For Annie Dillard

*Breathe fast: we are backing off the rim.*
　　　　　　— Annie Dillard, *Holy the Firm*


Your rim you see; your room you see:
window, glass wall, table round
as your cat's blue eye, and the mirror
of air, cored from rimless air,
offers mountain, island, forest,
sea.

If thought is a nun
who flexes in God's wake,
in the wake she christens God,
what does she wear when cold
cracks down, when the wake
spangles to abyss?

It's better not to write like this.
But you pass the handle and I grasp it.
Is there a choice?
Whose race is it
and why do we run?

It is Friday.
It is October.
It is raining
and I work beside a fire
in a yellow legal pad
without a back, your book
beside last Tuesday's wine.

It's rough to wake alone
and wean your eyes from bankless dark;
to salt your eggs alone
and single out the day.

Far simpler to dry the mug
and cross the road to town,
not noticing the pins of rain
that fasten to your hair
and tell you (if you hear)
that water is the only rim,
the only barrier. It's not.
I don't believe the rain.

Two days ago a man I knew
shot himself and his wife in my hometown.
The nun turned her habit inside out
and stood at a window facing north
until sun shred itself to coal;
until she could see no reflection in the pane,
could steal unnoticed in between
the paper and the pen.

Once, in your kitchen back east,
I watched you sketch a nun.
She was ugly, neckless, triangular,
stark. Maybe she's worked free of that;
maybe boundary has whetstoned her to arc.
Still, she stalks the oval entrance
to trees where owls freeze eyeless
and groundfrost stifles root.

Knots tighten in the novice's belt
as she swings translucent milk
in a wooden pail
and light spills emptily
to cover her intrusion
like a veil.

## The Poem

**I**

The poem
is its own
best brother.

It strains
round cells
against
the limber line.

It does not give
when tackled
but sticks, steep,
immovable, as fixed
as a stone's tall shade.

Walk around it carefully.
If you must touch it,
be prepared to ache.

**II**

It is like a river:
springs pull it taut;
if you break its surface
you distort your face.

If you try to cross
without your shoes
it takes you
down to its barbed bottom,
reveals to you
its sudden floor.

When you fear
for your own tricked breath
it will move to keep you:

your target bones
tell true tales
of the land,
its constant keeper,
its shadower grief.

## Rilke

Teach every play,
praises made of jugs and towers,
flowers breaking crooked stems
to prick your pale flesh,
rose dust, distant, into death.

I save my breath to speak your name.
It changes when I love.
Move me out again, dark brother.
Hold the other phrases back.
Knock to let me know you're here.

## For George Archibald

who courted Tex,
the whooping crane

### I

If you danced for her
and swung her heart
so skillfully
she offered you an egg,
how, afterward, did others sound —
the plainer breeds, committed fast
in lover nests, or those left
singular, unbound?

Waking nights,
did her eyes clamp you up
to dream over dream,
to feathered mansions
only flight-borne bodies know?
And could you fly — or whoop —
or lose your mind in air —
or was the dance
your single element,
the one true wilderness
where your heart
could unsuspected show?

### II

About this dance
I'm not so certain.
Something in the sight
of gulls or terns in fractured light
discovers doom
for those of us

who, ever after flight,
will try
against the given grain.

You've staked woe's death
in lost love's wildest game;
the feathers there are true;
true also is the smaller unaccustomed heart,
the heart she bears to brandish
in level awe of you.

Where here is betrayal?
Where loss,
where that starker grief
of lovers undefined
who must give in for regular ruin?
You dance.
She gives you what she can.

Without your cabin cages turn unsound —
audacity, bewilderment —
this love that finds no bound
whirls truest in air's elemental round.

Perhaps you dream of Daedalus; perhaps you don't.
Perhaps you'll never boast of your child's
perfect flight.
It makes no difference.
Only in the play of soul with feather soul,
only in this, the unlikeliest dance,
can dust-drawn creatures resurrect
the very need and nerve of chance.

# Air

For Bebe


Walk where we do
On whatever handprints
It's fundamental air
We share.

Air's what we gather
To give up
Most easily

What pulls words up
Or roots them
In space
Behind eyes
Other than our own

Eyes that see
Just far enough
To recognize
Relative blindness
Relative mortar
Relative bone

And
Within
Their kin.

# V Climbing Dead Man: Four Versions and a Solitary Climb

# Climbing Dead Man with Towles

For Towles Lawson

## I

Towles and I climb Dead Man.
Snow like ivy winds the trail.
In the whole spacious day
no cloud spins
and the cove
beyond boulders domed
like giant knees
sheers up in silver spools
to stop us.

Towles' ten years, ten shields,
surround to give him loft room.
I follow where he goes;
he shows me sycamores split
by lichen, deer prints, moss
so green it's black,
and the cross
pine shadows make
when the sun's wrong.

The trek down relieves us
of words' pressure.
When I trip I catch
my own curse at its latch.
Falls' simplicity reminds
me of the wealth in silence;
the wealth in stifling
even smallest comment
when things look back at you
on the way down.

## II

Towles ahead of me in rubber boots
tosses rocks.
I watch them: *fallen rocks.*
Blake celebrated sand grains,
other elemental miracles
among us like this air I take
and give away so easily
despite the sorriness of self.

Rocks trick down the trail
to meet my boots; I curse them,
curse imbalances, threats of fall.
I know them all I believe too well —

all but this one, this dearest one
through air too sheer to breathe,
to rock — all-stopping, other, all.

Still I follow rifts Towles leaves
and wish for Blake's huge heart
to help me learn to bless.
My mind spells words to friends
I've lasted out
and lost because of rock within;

and in this patience
not my own
I choose to balance
fright against the sheer lost fall-
ingness of rock and sand
and the wand of sunlight
through mountain pine,

each separate needle
before my eyes
driven haplessly
to gold.

## III

Towles is ten;
a score and five years, four yards
divide us as he spans
red-thistled mud to lead me up the trail
toward Dead Man's Skull.
Beside us woods crop close,
thin sunlight wreathes the leaves
and something live and out of sight
shifts underneath.

My breath goes straight, holds back.
Towles beyond the swerve of rock and grass
has reached the pass where once we saw
dead rabbits in a heap.
I hear his step,
I think about a book I read
called *Traces,* think,
*This, too, is one, a trace;*
*something in the air he's parted*
*stills the light and keeps it whole.*
*I fill that space.*

Air inside me stuns my throat,
and here, as I round the bend,
I feel the ghosts ascend
and circle upward, tolled by air.

Other shadows rush to steady.
Towles calls down to me,
                    "I'm there."

# IV

From Dead Man's Skull
we see three counties,
four shopping malls,
and the steeple of Christ's Church.
We straddle rocks, lean out
to place our selves.
Air too pure to take
lets our eyes see.

*If I were a tree,* I think;
*If I were a tree.*

Towles spins shale
out into emptiness,
and as it spills
another handful falls.
*Larger than dust,*
*is this just death*
*other-drawn,*
*made up for more?*

Here clouds hold no shape.
They change and spool,
come heavy, stretch and thin
into themselves.
Worlds below us move,
no more real
than panic I feel
in any space.

Here Towles traces letters in air.
I do not read them, can't.
I want my own.
More of us are shown,
by smaller things,
reasons to retrieve
descent; to dare.

## Dead Man Alone

When steepness starts
my heart denies me room
to breathe; years,
soul's weather thrall,
until I stop.

Below
the world is going
somewhere other.
Cars, cycles, men
in trucks carve direction —
pattern — red, green,
black, gold, blue, gray, or brown —
any color answers, any shade.

*Of this I too am made,*
I no more believe than say.
Yet even in denial
heart and blood respond.
Levels in me
rarely warmed by weather's light
shift, rescind

as the small oak
in William's meadow
takes its branches up
and weaves the wind.